BITE-SIZED
BOOKS

A Bite-Sized Business Book

Developing a Business Case

Making a Persuasive Argument out of Your Numbers

Paul Davies

ISBN: 9781521087602

Bite-Sized Books Ltd
Cleeve Croft, Cleeve Road, Goring RG8 9BJ UK
information@bite-sizedbooks.com
Registered in the UK. Company Registration No: 9395379

Contents

Introduction

Creating a business case is often confused with creating a business plan. The business case is usually a sub-set of the business plan and it has a different function from the plan and is designed to provide the essential financial information to support a business plan.

At its simplest, and in Microsoft Office terms, it is the Excel Spreadsheet to the plan's Word Document.

A business case is straightforward in its aim. Its whole purpose is to obtain the investment that a particular changed way of working requires. The investment can be in time, money or resources, or all three,

This **Bite-Sized Business Book** is designed to go to the heart of developing a business case, focusing on the essentials and it is a companion manual to the Bite-Sized Business Book, *Developing a Business Plan*.

It will give the reader a solid foundation for creating and developing a business case that will both achieve its purpose and meet the needs of several different audiences. Whatever the nature of the business you are working on and the type of business development you are analysing, this manual will give you the guidance you need.

A business case will reinforce the argument in your business plan and give the financial rationale for the business change. It may show, for example, a great return on investment, a way of protecting an existing revenue base, or an essential step that the business must take. To do this, the business case must change or reinforce the particular point of view of at least one individual.

As a result of a successfully approved business case, a business can usually obtain what it needs in terms of money and time to develop, change, advance, gain new revenue streams or exploit a new market with current products or services.

A business case, either on its own or as part of a business plan, should therefore be geared entirely around the objective of justifying the investment and commitment of the company to a new or revised direction.

A business case should err on the side of financial caution, anticipating higher costs than might be expected, and lower revenues. The intended audience or audiences will be more likely to approve a business case that represents the risks and the opportunities cautiously.

A business case should be as flexible as possible, so that all the costs and the revenues, the time lines and the outcomes are open to variation so a proper financial model that seems appropriate to all reviewers and approvers can be created and then modified over time. The objective is a valid document that underpins business development and isn't ignored once it has been accepted, but is continually revised in the light of changing circumstances.

Chapter 1

Version Control and Approval

Developing a business case is an iterative process and usually relies on collaboration across different disciplines within a company. It is vital to be able to track versions and levels of approval and we use two tables within the business plan to provide that tracking information:

- Version Control
- Approval.

Version Control is a table that records the following information:

- Which version, and we usually start with 0.1 until we have a distributed version, when we start using 1.0 and so on
- A description – for example "First draft"
- Status – for example "initial"
- Owner
- Comments
- Date of entry.

Approval is a table that records the following information:

- Version
- Level of sign off
- Name and role
- Signature(s)
- Date of entry in table.

Clearly you can adapt this to your own requirements, but you will find it is essential to be able to track different versions especially when the iterations are being shared more widely.

Chapter 2

Objectives, Flexibility, Assumptions, Audiences

There are many potential objectives for a business case including supporting the creation of a platform for business growth and development or defence of a revenue stream.

It is likely that the objectives will not be mutually exclusive and business cases have been designed both to gain investment from outside investors **and** to provide a solid platform from which to develop a sustainable new business.

This manual will give you an overview of the objectives you need to consider and how to address them effectively.

Flexibility

One of the key elements in any business case is making it sufficiently flexible so that reviewers and approvers can themselves try different inputs and see the results. This *what if* approach, where some data can be changed so those directly interested can see the effect of a different set of assumptions or suppositions, is also obviously very useful for you when developing a business case. You will quickly be able to see, for example, the effect of changes in recruitment profiles on profitability, time to being cash positive, and overall profitability.

You may find, for example, that increasing the number of customers for the business, especially one that is just starting, may not help profitability as support costs can go up disproportionately, or that increasing repeat business is less profitable because discount structures come into play.

To illustrate the first example consider this business which had to build a sophisticated customer support operation in anticipation of customer acquisition. In the early stages there was a large adverse step effect as for every twenty customers an extra three support staff had to be recruited, trained and deployed to give 24x7 capability. Every time we added one more customer over a multiple of twenty, we had a significant dip in profitability. Of course this was slightly artificial, as you can mitigate such effects in other ways, but it did help to show us that our initial marketing had to be at least as focused on getting repeat business as in acquiring customers.

While this was internally valuable, it was also highly persuasive when we were dealing with potential investors as it provided a proper justification for a whole range of decisions that we were making.

The value of spreadsheets in creating *what if* models is far too well known to labour, and all of this is fairly obvious, but it is often only with hindsight that people quite realise the value of building in the flexibility created in this approach to a business case. The approach can be perceived as complex and time consuming, but not taking this approach is quite soon even more time consuming and hardly straightforward, especially when you have to make inevitable adjustments to your numbers.

In short, this is a time warning – using this approach will mean that you will spend longer preparing the structure of your business case than you might anticipate, but that time is well spent.

Assumptions

Behind every business case there will be assumptions which can include, for example, the size of the market and the potential market, the pricing that can be achieved, the speed of take up of the product or service and the likely inflation rate that will apply differentially to supplies to the business and salary rates.

One of the most important parts of a business case is the nature and content of the assumptions and considerable thought should be given to making sure that the assumptions are both comprehensive and as justifiable as possible.

One reason for this statement is that every developer of a business case needs independent and reasoned feedback and criticism. It can usually be assumed that the person creating the business case will have the greatest knowledge about the financial environment within which the product or service must be successful. This means that a third party will not usually be able to challenge figures with any real authority, but what third parties can do is test the assumptions and see how the business case builds on, addresses or mitigates the effect of the assumptions.

Assumptions therefore become more and more important as the business case develops and is reviewed. In turn it is likely that more assumptions will be recorded as the development of the business case proceeds. You should therefore start by writing down what assumptions you are initially making and then add to them during the development process, removing those later that become irrelevant.

Audiences

As with any business document, whether you are a start-up, an established business or a global corporation, you need to decide who your audiences are for the business case and whether one single document can address all of them, or whether you need to modify the presentation of the figures to meet the various expectations and needs of different audiences. The basic financial information in the business case will not alter, but what you highlight and how you present the information might change.

It is unlikely that there will be one, homogenous audience. Being able to review your business case from a range of perspectives is important to you and the business and will inevitably make the document more effective.

This manual will help you identify and focus on the different audiences and decide which your main priorities are. Typical audiences include:

- All direct stakeholders
  - Shareholders
  - The Board, including non-executive directors
  - The senior management
  - The staff
  - Pensioners of the company
- Potential investors
- Potential employees
- Business partners and companies that you may have formed a consortium with.

This is not an exhaustive list, but it is usually helpful to identify the audience or audiences and then focus on the particular interests that you must address to gain their buy in to your case.

Chapter 3

Starting Planning

The starting point of any business plan and, by extension any business case, is the initial idea or proposition, whether this is, for example, a new product or service, a revised approach to current products and services, a different way of segmenting the market or creating a faster growth strategy.

To create any business case, you will need to gather a range of information, mostly financial, that will help you put together a rationale to support the business proposition. You will also draw on a great deal of information already in the business plan, particularly around any competitive information and market data.

As you gather this data, you will also begin to understand more of the assumptions you are making.

There are various elements in the business plan that can be incorporated under the business case heading, for example the competitive analysis. There is no right or wrong answer to the question of what should also be included in the business case beyond what is advocated here. Nevertheless, separating out segments from the business case, such as the competitive analysis and market size, will make it easier to get started and create the main thrust of your argument.

This Bite-Sized Business Book provides you with an effective framework in which to display your financial data and support the financial argument that you want to make and is totally focused on gaining the approval you need to continue your new business direction.

The Process

This book is focused on developing the right framework for an effective business case. You will need to add the actual figures once you have constructed the model.

You will have a range of financial information at your fingertips already, but you will need more in order to populate the business case you are developing. This business case format will prompt you about the further information you require

Each individual business case will require different areas of focus and do modify the structure where that seems appropriate to you. This is a framework not a straitjacket.

In short, this approach is comprehensive without being exhaustive and once you have the framework, the real modelling can begin.

Labelling

There are conventions here that you may find valuable.

Year 0

Year 0 – zero – is often used for the time before revenue but after costs have started to be incurred. In practice it has limited use, but some business cases are based on a view that when revenues start to flow, the whole approach will change.

This is particularly true where there is a large initial investment required, in, for example, tooling, the recruitment and training of staff, or software development. The advantage of the Year 0 approach is that it highlights the level of risk that is being taken on. The Year 0 approach can readily be incorporated into this business case format, by adding an extra column – see below.

Year 0 can obviously be less than twelve months and might only be, for example, a quarter.

Years 1, 2 and 3

It is becoming increasingly difficult to create a business case that extends beyond Year 3. The world is changing so fast now, in technology, regulations, and international relations, to name but three, that looking further than 36 months ahead is usually challenging.

In even more changeable markets, it is best to create an indicative 36 month business case, with a much more realistic focus on a rolling twelve month planning horizon. That is every month, the business case is updated to look in detail at the next twelve months. (Some companies update it quarterly.)

Nevertheless, this manual looks at a standard 36 month business case and we use the appropriate labels, preferring not to name the months, but calling them Month 1 through Month 36. It is a fact that things slip and are rarely brought forward, so it is best to number the months in your business case.

Review

An essential element in the development of a business case is to build in a review process so that the document does not become electronic concrete – set and forgotten. The review process is outside the scope of this document, as it usually relates to company policy and procedures, but it should be considered at a relatively early stage in the development of the business case. The sooner you start to get internal feedback the better the final business case will be.

Any business case will benefit from discussion by a range of interested and disinterested reviewers during its development.

For the longer term, it is also good practice to utilise the knowledge and understanding built up during the development phase when you are implementing the business plan and case.

Perfection

All business cases are imperfect in some ways, and will use rounding up and approximations at various points. The real world will not quite function like the business case you produce. As minor examples, not every employee will start on day one of a particular month and service or product delivery may well not take place immediately an order is received. In short, there will be compromises.

The justification for not achieving perfection is that while every business case will have rough edges, the general thrust and overall results will be as close to actuality as necessary for your purposes. The objective of a business case is not to produce the perfect, all singing, all dancing business case but to create as reasonably accurate a statement of the likely financial outcomes as is sensible, and one that you can put your name to as justifiable.

There will be no right or wrong answer to how much time you spend getting the most accurate answer only what is appropriate to your own particular concerns and the financial sensitivities of the business you are in.

Excel

It is more than likely that you will use Excel[1] to develop your business case. This **Bite-Sized Book** cannot provide training in using Excel, which is

---

[1] The Microsoft Office Spreadsheet Programme

both a multi-faceted, complex programme and also relatively simple to use at the most basic levels.

There are two elements, however, that will be extremely important to you that we want to stress, as you start to link the various cells in the different sheets within one workbook.

If you merely want to paste the results of a calculation in a different sheet, say in **Summary** from the **Costs** sheet, then you can use the Excel *paste link* feature. *Copy* the origin cell and then use *paste link* to create the target cell. Every time you change the origin cell, you will update the linked cell.

If you want to create a calculated result in a cell, then you can use the standard function *=sum()*. Write *=sum(* in the destination cell, then go to the first cell you want to calculate from, click on it, then apply an action, *+, -, / or ** , and then go to the cell you want to complete the calculation with, which can be in a different sheet, and click on that. Every time you change one of the underlying numbers, probably in the **Data Entry** sheet, Excel will either automatically recalculate the results or do so when you force it to update.

Chapter 4
Business Case Components

Here we look at the components of a business case in detail and how to build the components into complete business case. We start by looking at the structure of a business case, giving an outline of the content, and then explain each of the components that we think are significant in creating the argument for the investment you are seeking.

A business case is not a complete set of accounts, but a demonstration of what your best insights suggest will happen to the business that you are building. To illustrate the difference, a full set of accounts for a business, which are generally produced looking backwards at what has happened, will include a balance sheet. This balance sheet will show you a full picture of the business at a particular point in time, showing the assets and the liabilities. A balance sheet can sometimes be created for a business case, but there is little point. The significant elements of the business case are whether the business will be profitable and how quickly, and also what the cash and investment requirements will be.

The aim is to produce a business case that shows what costs are going to be incurred, how revenues are going to be built up, how profitable the business will be and in what space of time.

The business case focused on in this Bite-Sized Business Manual does just that.

Designing and building the individual sheets is one stage, and that is covered by this manual. Data entry, where you put in the actual numbers, can occur any time after you have started to build your business case.

Outline

Every business case will be different in content but similar in form. The sheets that we suggest for the business case workbook are:

- Summary
- Profit and Loss
- Cash flow
- Revenue

- Staffing – numbers
- Staffing – costs
- Overall costs
- Data
- Data Entry
- Assumptions.

Possibly not all will be required in every case, but each component is valuable in its own way for particular audiences.

The summary will probably be the last sheet that you build even though it will be presented first.

The segments will be addressed in the initial order you will find best.

You can see that the **Staffing** sheet is divided into two. It can be handled in one, but it is much clearer and therefore more effective to divide the staffing sheet into the one which gives the numbers of staff in each category month by month and another which gives the staff costs month by month. It is also a good deal simpler like that when combining all the costs

You may also find it useful to have a statement of the *purpose* of the business case on the **Summary** sheet – see the next sub-heading.

In creating this structure the idea is to make a narrative that is relatively easy to understand, and that is why the **Summary** is the most important part of the way you present the information.

Each of the components above are broken down and explained under their individual headings below, in the order that you will initially address them.

Purpose

We find it useful to remind clients why the business case is being produced and your reviewers and approvers will find a succinct statement of the purpose of the document will help them assimilate the information and place it in context. We suggest that this should be a heading in the **Summary** sheet, a cover note or at least a part of the email or message that you use to distribute the business case.

This approach will also help you concentrate on what is relevant.

In all cases you are seeking to change at least one person's perception of the current or future business so that you can make a business stronger, more effective, more sustainable and more profitable.

The purpose of the business case is to demonstrate to the business and interested parties the financial effects of the changes that a business plan is advocating.

There are a number of reasons why a business case is required, so it is usually not a question of stating one purpose, but of encompassing all the reasons.

The purpose issues that we have generally found valuable include:

- New investment is required for a new business, a new business idea, a new approach to the market or to build on a successful business
- It is necessary to ensure that all decision makers and influencers within a business understand the strategy and have the chance to test the reasons for the new strategy, and then the company can go forward with some unanimity
- Regulatory changes have forced the business to re-evaluate how it goes to market and the business case encapsulates the financial effects of the changes you are proposing
- Other external events, such as a recession, technological changes, potential conflicts, shortages of supplies of components, raw materials or energy sources mean that the business has to change
- An internal re-organisation requires the company to operate in a different way and it is necessary to examine all areas in a logical and rational way so that pitfalls can be avoided.

Here is a specific example of the **purpose** component:

> *The purpose of this business case is to demonstrate the financial impact of adopting the changes that are proposed in the [relevant] business plan and to provide a mechanism to explore a variety of different assumptions and outcomes.*

Assumptions

We have found that the following areas are at least influenced by assumptions that business planners have had to make, and it is usually important to consider whether you have made assumptions in these areas, and to describe them:

- The direction of input prices to your business, including raw materials, energy, components, and local taxes

- Staff costs, including salaries, attrition rates
- Recruitment profiles and dates
- The risk profile your company employs
- Price movements in the market for your products and services
- Elasticity of demand
- Market changes, including interest rates, ability to raise finance
- Macro-economic movements, such as recession, booms
- Regulatory changes
- International factors, including conflicts
- Growth in market size
- Changes in markets
- Changes in technology – are you sure, for example, that there is no disruptive technology that will undermine your business case almost immediately
- New channels to market – look at the rise in mobile commerce
- Government policies and potential changes
- Acceptability of products
- Changes in attitudes
- Environmental issues.

It would be wrong to suggest that the key to a successful business case is a full and open statement of the assumptions behind the development but it is the key to gaining wider acceptance and a more positive response to your document.

If people realise that the plan is based on overt and what they consider are correct assumptions, it gives far more credibility to your document.

As the purpose of the document is to change perceptions and gain buy-in, the importance of the assumptions seems obvious.

Data

The **Data** sheet is the repository of most of the data that is going to be in your business case and it will be *pasted* and *paste linked* into the relevant sheets as and when required.

This is the first section with which to begin building a business case as it is generally straightforward.

It is relatively easy to identify what types of data should be included, even if you do not manage to cover all the areas at your first attempt.

Most of the information and numbers that are in the **Data** sheet will be input one way or another as fixed numbers.

There will be some calculated fields in the **Data** sheet but this is for convenience when populating the other sheets, like the **Profit and Loss** sheet. The best example of this is when calculating full staff costs. You may, for example, have separate entries for the base salary, social costs, benefits, and pensions. When you have to use the full cost of employees in each category, it is much easier to have these various entries totalled in the **Data** sheet as well as broken down into elements of the cost.

There is a separate sheet called **Data Entry** which does what it says on the label. You will find that there is some data that you rarely want to alter or adjust, even to do a *what if* analysis. Using a separate **Data Entry** sheet will stop you inadvertently making changes to data that you want to keep intact, and allows you to protect the **Data** sheet from such changes. See below for more information under the heading **Data Entry**.

Do note that in the list of entries for the **Data** sheet, the idea is to future proof the business case. For example, you will see that there are five levels of employee below in each department, and each level is given a separate salary level. You may find that five levels is too much, but it is easier to ignore a row in the sheet than to interpolate one at a later stage.

Please err on the side of caution here, having more levels than you need is better than having to shoe horn an extra entry into your sheet.

Therefore where you see a number next to a category in the example below, for example *Customer Type 1*, do not confuse this with the idea of the first customer – it is a *type* of customer or client.

The more different levels of granularity that you apply to each part of the data will make the design of the spreadsheet easier, but it will make it more complex to work with and make it more difficult to see the overall picture. It is a fine balance, and you will find the right level of complexity.

We provide either Year 0 to Year 3 in the columns or Year 1 to Year 3 and a further column to the right. (This is usually useful for notes, but it can also be used for totals, where this is appropriate.)

This example shows the way we write the table for a Year 1 to Year 3 business case:

Items	Y1	Y2	Y3	Total/Comments
Clients				
Client Type 1 # added by end of year (C1)	5	12	15	32
Client Type 2 # added by end of year (C2)	4	0	12	26
Client Type 3 # added by end of year (C3)	3	5	8	16
Client Type 4 # added by end of year (C4)	2	5	7	14
Client Type 5 # added by end of year (C5)	1	3	4	8

The following is a list of the top level categories in the **Data** sheet:

- Product and services data
- Client data
- Supplier data
- Staff costs
- Office costs
- IT costs
- Other costs
- Computation data.

Product and Services Data

You will have an understanding of how many products and how many service lines you have, and, depending upon the level of granularity you want to achieve, you should have a row for each. In turn you may want separate blocks for the following:

- Product cost – if you have the right information
- Product price
- Service cost – if this is not included in staff costs below
- Service price.

This is simplest for products that you buy in and re-sell, but often the product cost is made up of a number of components, some bought in and some developed in-house. If the in-house costs are mainly staff time and office or factory space, this cost will already be included elsewhere and it is important not to double count. Nevertheless, you may want to compute the product cost and should create a separate block in which to do so.

The simpler table you create can look like this:

Items	Y1	Y2	Y3	Total/Comments
Products - Price				
$Product 1	230.00	241.50	253.58	
$Product 2	270.00	283.50	297.68	
$Product 3	300.00	315.00	330.75	
$Product 4	450.00	472.50	496.13	
$Product 5	500.00	525.00	551.25	
Products - Cost				
$Product 1	184.00	193.20	202.86	
$Product 2	216.00	226.80	238.14	
$Product 3	240.00	252.00	264.60	
$Product 4	360.00	378.00	396.90	
$Product 5	400.00	420.00	441.00	

Client Data

When refining a business case it is useful to have different segments of clients or customers. We find that five types usually is sufficient, as we showed above.

The basis for the segmentation can be in a number of different ways, for example, it can be on the total revenue each has, but we tend to use the measure of the size of each individual order we can expect. At this stage you do not need to decide what the boundaries are.

We then have a further data point for each of the up to five types of customers, which is based on the number of times we can expect the customer to buy in a year.

Finally we have the same number of customer types and we do not label this yet, but use it as a safeguard in case we need to categorise the types of customers in a different way later on.

Supplier Data

You should also provide the same information about suppliers of either components or raw materials to the business. There are different entries for stationery and utilities for example.

You may have a range of business suppliers for raw materials, transportation, distribution and components. Again it is useful to provide a range of supplier types, possibly, depending on your type of business, providing for different types or levels of a category of suppliers.

We use the same grid and layout as in the examples above.

Staff Costs

First of all divide the senior management team from the rest of the staff and identify them individually, using the same table grid as above.

One jargon way of representing this level of management is *CXO*, where the *X* stands for the changing function – say CEO standing for C *Executive* O or CFO standing for C *Finance* O.

Compute the cost to the project based on the amount of time we assume each will be giving to the business under consideration. (That percentage figure is held in the **Computation Data** section below.)

You will know how many people to identify here, but using the Chief Officer denomination it could be:

- CEO – Chief Executive
- COO – Chief Operating
- CFO – Chief Finance
- CIO – Chief Information
- CMO – Chief Marketing.

Then list each department and give up to five levels of staff within each department, depending on how flat your organisation is.

The types of department differ but here is a representative list that you can adapt to your specific requirements:

- Finance
- Administration
- Sales
- Marketing
- Customer Consultancy
- Customer Support
- Project and Programme Management
- HR
- IT
- IT Support
- Support Services – distribution for example
- Outsourced costs – very often payroll, for example.

With staff there is usually a base salary cost, but on top of that there will be social costs, pensions and any other benefits. It is useful to quote the base salary and have a different table entry for each of the benefits, and then finally compute a full year cost for each category.

It isn't necessary to do it this way, but it is a great deal clearer and therefore easier to understand, and also approvers and reviewers will probably be used to seeing the salary cost without the additional costs and helps them see how the costs are built up in a more understandable way.

Depending upon your country, social costs, for example, can usually be calculated relative to salary, as can pension costs over and above what an employee contributes.

You may tie the number of, for example, IT Support Staff to the overall number of employees. This may be a level of sophistication that is unnecessary for you, but it is worth considering.

If you are going to do this, you need to add another row in the Computation Data with the ratio that you anticipate using for each of these roles. The roles that can be varied like this include all support staff and HR.

Do be aware that you can create an endless, iterative circle here, as you may relate the number of admin staff to the number of overall staff which is itself a total of all staff including admin staff.

Our advice here is to go for simplicity and only use the calculated method for one or two roles and adjust the number of other staff manually, see below in the **Staffing** sheet.

Office Costs

There are essentially two types of office costs:

- Capital costs – furniture for example
- Monthly or recurring expenditure.

You should always show the costs as they are incurred, in order to make the cash flow more accurate. Give the costs in the **Data** sheet as a figure per employee, and make this clear in the Total/Comments column, so when we recruit a new office worker we have the capital cost of furniture, for example, immediately applied to the costs.

We also tie monthly expenditure to the number of employees where this is appropriate. For example you can make the cost of utilities proportionate to the number of employees.

Office space, however, should be treated differently, as you cannot realistically increment office space each time a new employee starts. Although this will probably overstate office costs, work out how many staff you will have at the end of the three year period and allow office space for the whole complement, and base your rent and local taxes on that full cost. This will overstate the cost as it is perfectly possible to take offices big enough for the first year and then add to them, and this is probably what you will do in practice. On the other hand, you will show how conservative you are in working out costs, and that always impresses reviewers and approvers.

The items under **Office Costs** include:

- Rent per month for the whole office space
- Business rates or local authority taxes for the whole office space
- Utilities per employee
- Telecoms per employee
- Internet per employee
- Printing per employee
- Postage
- Staff expenses – per employee
- Furniture cost per employee
- Furniture cost – non-employee related
- IT cost per employee
- Dilapidations per square foot
- Miscellaneous per employee
- Professional services – accountancy
- Professional services – legal
- Professional services – consultancy
- Bank and finance charges.

The IT costs per employee here are not for central systems but the costs for each individual's laptop or table and associated costs.

You will find it useful to have the miscellaneous line, as there will often be some costs which you have managed to omit.

It is difficult to estimate professional services, accountants, lawyers and consultants, but it is essential to include these as cost lines. Breaking down professional services into three elements helps in the creation of justifiable figures.

Your bank and finance charges can be worked out or estimated and should be included.

Dilapidations are often forgotten but are usually a cost that you should accrue for when taking out a lease for offices. Your leasing agreement should show you what to allow.

IT Costs

The IT cost is the central system. These can be leased or will be provided through the cloud and so are usually now a monthly cost and are best dealt with as a monthly cost.

Depending upon your circumstances you can either make this a fixed amount spread over the period of the business case or you can make it relative to the number of employees. Neither way will be totally accurate and the latter approach does show how costs increase relative to the growth of the company or business unit.

Other Costs

There will be a range of other costs to consider, and the most significant to consider are these two:

- Training
- Recruitment.

In practice with a new business, training is very often part of the sunk cost of employing someone, as no external training resources are used. It is, however, appropriate to add a figure for training per employee per annum, even if this is relatively minor. As your business grows, there will be need for more training and that will inevitably mean costs.

Initial recruitment for a small business or start-up will no doubt be by word of mouth, but it is likely that fairly soon there will be recruitment costs per employee. When estimating these, do not underestimate the costs, as recruitment is never a straightforward linear process of advertisement, long list, short list, appointment. There may well be a number of iterations, as candidates refuse the offer, change their minds or make different demands.

Outsourced Costs

These are relatively easy to identify and they will usually be sensitive to volume, say the number of employees on the payroll.

Computation Data

There are a number of variables that you will want to be able to define and include in your calculated results, and the obvious ones are inflation rates for salaries, for supplies and for your pricing. (We tend to ignore the latter as we always aim to create a pessimistic statement of revenue.)

Some of the variables below depend on the size of your company or business unit, so, for example, if your CEO is full time on this particular business opportunity, there will be no overhead cost, just the full cost. Where the CEO has some engagement with the project or programme, then you will ideally indicate a figure for how much of his or her cost should be allocated to the business case.

The following are some of the computation data issues to consider:

- How much time each CXO spends on the project or business focus
- Inflation rates for each year – salaries
- Inflation rates for each year – supplies
- Inflation rates for each year – pricing
- Finance interest rates
- Staff attrition rates
- Number of deals each sales person can complete a month – perhaps broken down by size of customer
- How many square feet or square metres are allowed per member of staff, building in a contingency figure for break out and kitchen space,
- Ratio of support staff to other employees
- Ratio of IT support staff to other employees
- Anticipated sales growth per annum.

The final item may not be used for developing revenue figures but it can act as a sense check on your sales figures. For a start-up, for example, it is not unreasonable to expect 100% growth rates, from a low base. For an existing business following a new path, it is unlikely that sales growth will exceed 20%, unless there are strong factors that suggest otherwise.

While not exactly computational data, it is often useful to record other data items, such as sales cycle length, delivery cycles and time between employing sales staff and recording their first sale. When constructing the **Revenue** sheet, it will help justify revenue amounts you posit.

Chapter 5

The Separate Work Sheets

Data Sheet

As we have explained, it is useful to *protect* the **Data** sheet so that no entries can be inadvertently over-written, as much of the data will not be subject to change. This is an inbuilt function of Excel.

To make this a practical approach, use a copy of the **Data** sheet as a **Data Entry** sheet, only keeping the rows that will be most often changed, either to reflect different or updated information or when doing a *what if* analysis.

There are two refinements you should consider, one procedural and one useful.

The procedural one is to make sure that you establish a base version of the business case and that each time you make changes with the **Data Entry** sheet, you update the **Version Control** table and save the business case with a different version number. This means that you can always go back to the base figures that you are currently using – which will change over the development time, of course.

The useful one is to create a sort of *ready reckoner* on the Data Entry sheet so you can easily see the results of any changes you make. The ready reckoner should be relatively simple and one is example is the table below, where the figures are from an actual business case:

Ready Reckoner				
	Y1	Y2	Y3	Total
Total costs	1,054,559.17	1,987,017.08	3,598,917.37	6,640,493.62
Total income	199,200.00	1,020,000.00	6,357,728.00	7,576,928.00
Profit/Loss	-855,359.17	-967,017.08	2,758,810.63	936,434.38

As you change any of your data, the results will ripple through the spreadsheet and give you an indication of what effect you are producing.

Staffing Sheet

Encapsulating staff numbers and costs can be awkward, and you should take a simple, though painstaking approach.

Create a table with each of 36 months as the column headings, assuming a three year business case. The first row should contain entries for all the different roles that you have envisaged in the **Data** sheet. It is a good deal easier if you have over-estimated the number of roles in that sheet, because it is simpler to ignore than to shoe horn in an extra set of figures.

For most of the roles, it is merely sensible to put in to each relevant cell the number of staff members that you anticipate you will have in that role at any particular time. This simple table illustrates what we mean:

	0	1	2	3	4	5
CEO		1	1	1	1	1
COO		0	0	0	0	0
CFO		0	0	0	1	1
CIO		0	0	0	1	1
CMO		0	0	0	0	0
Member support		1	1	1	5	5
Client support		1	1	1	4	4
Sales people		0	0	0	1	1
Marketing		0	1	1	1	1
Finance		0	0	0	1	1
Administration		0	0	0	1	1
IT Team Leader		1	1	1	1	1
Software developers		2	2	2	2	2
Software testers		1	1	1	1	1
Tech support		2	2	2	2	2
HR		0.50	0.50	0.50	0.50	0.50

The exception to this approach are those that are computed, for example if you have decided that the number of IT support staff is proportional to the number of staff. In such a case you will need to know the total number of staff for each month and then divide by the figure in the **Data** sheet that tells you how many IT Support staff there are per full time employee and round that figure up to a whole number.

In the final row, you should total the number of staff per month. If you have a number of roles with variable numbers based on the number of other staff, as above with the IT Support Staff, you should have a row which shows the total number of staff minus the variable ones.

Overall Costs

In the **Data** sheet, the majority of the costs that will be included have been identified – you may find your particular circumstances mean that there are further costs not covered here. You now need to turn that data into information.

Although it is painstaking and can appear to be slow, it is useful to break the costs down to each of the 36 months – assuming that that is the period covered by your business case.

You then need to have a row for each of the cost lines that you want to include, some of which will be computed from two or more data sheets. For example you know the total salary cost for each type of staff member and in the **Staffing** sheet, see above, you will have the numbers of staff employed within that function each month.

Ensure that you understand which of the cost items are related to staff numbers and calculate the cost automatically using formulae. These include furniture costs and individual IT costs, for example.

It is slightly more difficult if you take the furniture, for example, as a capital cost each time a new employee joins as opposed to spreading the cost over the three years of the business case, but not a difficult formula to create.

Below the rows of costs, it is useful to have the total monthly cost for the whole business, not only for the value of the information but also as a sort of checksum that you haven't inadvertently mis-typed some figures, as there should be a steady progression through the totals and if there are anomalies these will stand out immediately.

If you haven't provided for the full office space for the 36 months at the outset and seek to expand space at the end of each year, then this will need to be computed.

Some of the costs other than staffing costs will be dependent upon the staff numbers, so you will have to get the relevant figures from the **Staffing** sheet.

You will also have to allow for inflation, using the **Computation Data** sheet, presumably at the beginning of each twelve month period.

The recruitment costs, which we suggest may be minimal, certainly in the first six months and perhaps for the first twelve months, have to be built in in two ways:

- The cost per new member of staff
- The cost for new members of staff that are there to replace the existing staff who have left – you use the **Attrition Rate** in the Data

sheet to determine the leavers, rounding up to the nearest whole number.

Training costs may not apply to all members of staff, but we find that assuming they do is more realistic or, at least, pessimistic, which is what we prefer in totalling the costs.

The usual mistake that is made creating this table is confusing whether there are monthly or annual costs being entered in the monthly columns, so please be careful when creating the calculation.

You will find that the costs will jump at the end of each year as figures for inflation change the calculations and there are other side effects of the way the business case is constructed, but they usually do not affect the argument that underlies the figures.

You will also find it useful to have a small table below that major table, where you can summarise the costs, broken down in as much detail as you prefer or need, for each year. It is often useful, for example, to have a line just devoted to staff costs.

Revenue Sheet

Revenue is not cash, as you no doubt know, but it is income recognised for accounting purposes when you legally invoice a customer or client.

Again we use the same 36 month table, identifying each of the products and services and anticipating the revenue that can be derived, against the types of customer, as this table shows:

	0	1	2	3	4	5
C1		2,500.00	2,500.00	2,500.00	2,500.00	2,500.00
C2		2,666.67	2,666.67	2,666.67	2,666.67	2,666.67
C3		1,800.00	1,800.00	1,800.00	1,800.00	1,800.00
C4		1,000.00	1,000.00	1,000.00	1,000.00	1,000.00
C5		333.33	333.33	333.33	333.33	333.33

It is particularly important to consider the extra information you placed in the **Computational Data** sheet about length of sales cycle and other factors such as time before a sales person becomes effective. (This is usually the justification for having the Year 0 column, where you have all the costs and no revenue.)

If you are going to use the spreadsheet to calculate the revenue automatically, relating it, for example, to the number of clients, their propensity to place an order, and knowing the average value of each order, it may be best to break down the revenue table into rows for each of the types of customer or client, as above.

Revenue can also automatically be calculated from the number of sales people. In fact, it is often useful to identify what number of sales are required from each sales person as a sanity check on your expectations.

It is unlikely that you can assume any revenues from earlier than month 3, unless you have a strong justification.

Finally, do remember that there are rules for when you can recognise revenue, and this will be a contractual issue. It can be, for example, that you will work to contracts that specify staged payments against staged delivery or services rendered each month that can be invoiced at the end of that relevant month. It can be that you cannot invoice until a complete delivery is finished. Obviously you are not preparing the company's accounts, but it is sensible to apply the same standards.

You are strongly advised to be highly conservative recognising revenue when you are developing your business case, and ensure that you build in contingency. Just as it is rare for any recruitment process to be smooth and sequential, so it is unlikely that every order will follow the right pattern and provide you with revenue in quite the way you ought to be able to expect.

Cash flow Sheet

It is often said that cash is king and this is one of the most important sheets in the business case workbook.

This sheet is the one that will tell you how much you have to borrow to finance the business before it becomes cash positive and then profitable. In this context, cash positive means when a month actually has more cash coming in than is going out; being profitable is the moment when the business has taken more revenue than its costs to date have been.

As any developer of a business case knows, cash follows revenue. This will be a contractual issue and the payment period will usually be stipulated. You can usually anticipate a 30 day payment cycle, but large companies especially can be the worst culprits in using start-ups and small businesses as involuntary banks, forcing the small companies to lend them money for 42 days or 60 days.

Using the same 36 month chart, you can keep the costs exactly as they are in the **Overall Costs** sheets – an opportunity to use *paste link*.

The simplest way of establishing the cash position each month is to transpose the revenue by one month later or whatever the payment terms are that you anticipate. As you work on the business case, you can refine this. Here you will typically use the *=sum()* function mentioned earlier.

The most important element of the **Cash Flow** sheet is where you total the various amounts per month.

In the first row of totals at the bottom of the sheet, identify the position at the end of every month by totalling the figures above which include both revenue and costs. This row will show you when the business becomes cash positive on a month by month basis.

Below that row, create an accumulated total to date showing the net cash position. Do this by adding the second month to the first month's outcome, then the third month's outcome to that – and so on. There will probably be a loss for at least the first year. There will – or should – come a point where this figure becomes positive and this is when your business is *cash profitable*.

The real importance of this row, however, is that it should predict the highest amount of cash that you need to sustain the business, and therefore the financial investment you require, and by when you will need it.

Profit and Loss

This is a similar sheet to the **Cash Flow** sheet, except that it is based on revenue and costs as opposed to cash and costs.

Create a similar sheet with the 36 month column layout but you need as little as two rows plus a total. (You may want to make it more sophisticated, and there are suggestions below.) The two rows are:

- Total costs per month
- Total revenue per month.

Underneath that there will be a row for the total outcome per month, and, again, you can create an accumulated position, just like the **Cash Flow** sheet.

You may wish to break the costs down into the components we used in the **Data** sheet:

- Product and services
- Client

- Supplier
- Staff
- Office
- IT
- Other.

You may also wish to break down the revenue lines into different product areas. We tend to aim for simplicity in this sheet as the story it tells is more important than the details, and all the details are available elsewhere.

Summary Sheet

In the **Summary** sheet, we usually have two tables:

- One showing the outcomes for the three years
- One showing the outcomes for the twelve quarters.

For good reasons, many reviewers and approvers of business cases do like to see the staff costs broken out on the **Summary** sheet.

What the sheet is designed to show is a quick overview of how the business is going to develop over the chosen time span – in our example three years.

If this sheet does not tell the right story to support your business plan, it is unlikely that the business plan will be approved.

As we suggested earlier, if there is a major investment up front, it may be that you will have to develop a five year plan, using 60 months instead of 36, as this will allow you to amortise the costs over a longer period.

On the other hand, this Summary may just tell you that this is not a good proposition as it stands and that you need to go back a few stages, not necessarily to stage 1, and reconsider how your costs build up and what you might have to do to build revenues earlier.

Chapter 6

Integration with the Business Plan

In developing the Business Case we have considered:

- Assumptions about financial matters, such as interest rates, differential inflation rates (for, say, salaries and raw materials), contingency, and how optimistic or pessimistic the assumptions are
- Costs – and whether you should consider a pre-revenue approach, the Year 0 method
- Costs post launch
  - How they build up
  - Time scales for them to increase
- Revenues and how they build up over time
- Cash flow – particularly important when considering what investment is needed
- The profit and loss account
- The balance sheet – but suggested that this is irrelevant for most Business Cases
- The overall summary which will include the projected results over three years (or whatever period is chosen).

What is required in the Business Plan is:

- The overall summary
- Time to revenue
- Time to being cash positive
- Time to profitability
- What percentage market share of the total market you have identified you will achieve.

Each of these, apart from the last, can be *paste link*ed into the Business Plan.

With this information readily at hand, most reviewers and approvers of the Business Case will have enough information to take a view. This is a vital first step to getting the Business Plan approved.

Nearly all will want to study your actual business case in more detail, so that they can understand how rigorous you have been, how conservative in working out revenue growth and whether you have adequately covered all likely costs.

It is usually a good idea to add a picture of how the costs build up quarter by quarter and how revenues increase in the same time periods.

The business plan will have some information about the overall size of the market that you are aiming at, and you will find it useful to show what percentage of this overall market you expect to achieve at the end of the business plan and case period.

The business plan will be built upon the supposition that you need to gain something like 30% of the defined target market in order to be profitable if it is a mature market. This does depend on how you segment your market, but this should be borne in mind.

Chapter 7

Next Steps

Now you will have to populate the **Data** sheet, check that all the links work and check also that the logic you have applied works. When you are effectively debugging your Business Case, you will find odd spikes in costs and revenue, some caused by the method we have chosen but some will be down to errors you have introduced into the links, and you will find anomalies in the way the cash flow works. This is where the Data Entry sheet comes into its own and the *what if* approach will help, because you can enter data and see how it affects the outcomes, and usually more readily see where the issues are with your calculations and links.

We always find that you should take a third party who has not been involved in developing the Business Case through the whole Business Case, explaining how the links work and what you have done and how you have addressed timing and other issues.

They actually won't see any issues but you will.

Counter-intuitive but true.

Chapter 8

Conclusion

What we have described here is the framework or template for a Business Case and how to develop, arrange and link the numbers and information.

As you will no doubt have gathered, researching and assembling the data in the right place is much more of a task, but equipping people with the right mind set and framework considerably improves the chances of successful development of a Business Case and the successful approval of a Business Plan.

The advantage of the **Data** sheet as conceived here is that it focuses you on what information you need and in what format.

Please remember that the objective is not to create the perfect Business Case but to have a Business Case that supports your Business Plan and allows you to gain the investment approval so that you can achieve your business aims.

Finally, don't think you have to complete the Business Case in the order of the components that we have given – in fact you may find that impossible.

See the Business Case as an iterative process that will enable you to achieve the business benefits your proposed investment is focused on. Develop the components that you need in the order that is logical to you.

Once you have won approval, keep the Business Case with you both to check your progress against what you planned and also to help you create a better, more accurate and comprehensive Business Case next time.

BITE-SIZED
BOOKS

The most successful people all share an ability to focus on what really matters, keeping things understandable and simple. MBAs, metrics and methodologies have their place, but when we are faced with a new business challenge most of us need quick guidance on what matters most, from people who have been there before and who can show us where to start. As Stephen Covey famously said, "The main thing is to keep the main thing, the main thing".

But what exactly is the main thing?

We created Bite-Sized books to help answer precisely that question crisply and quickly, working with writers who are experienced, successful and, of course, engaging to read.

The brief? Distil the *main things* into a book that can be read by an intelligent non-expert comfortably in around 60 minutes. Make sure the book provides the reader with specific tools, ideas and plenty of examples drawn from real life and business. Be a virtual mentor.

Bite-Sized Books don't cover every eventuality, but they are written from the heart by successful people who are happy to share their experience with you and give you the benefit of their success.

Printed in Great Britain
by Amazon

81473608R00031